Cacti as Decorative Plants

Cacti as Decorative Plants

JACK KRAMER

Drawings by Michael Valdez
(unless otherwise stated)

CHARLES SCRIBNER'S SONS · New York

LIBRARY OF CONGRESS CATALOGING IN PUBLICATION DATA

Kramer, Jack, 1927-
    Cacti as decorative plants.

    Bibliography: p.
    1. Cactus.   I. Title
SB438.K7   635.9′34′7   73-17269

        ISBN 0-684-13702-X
        ISBN 0-684-13718-6 (pkb)

1 3 5 7 9 11 13 15 17 19 MD/C 20 18 16 14 12 10 8 6 4 2
    3 5 7 9 11 13 15 17 19 M/C 20 18 16 14 12 10 8 6 4 2

Printed in the United States of America

Contents

Cacti as Decorative Plants

Introduction:
Decorating with Cacti

Treelike plants such as *Dieffenbachias* and *Ficus Benjamina*, large palms and ferns are all part of today's contemporary room settings. Indeed, you never see a magazine photo of a room without some plants. Recently, an age-old group of plants—Cactaceae—that for years had been considered hobbyist's plants, have appeared indoors as decorative accessories, and with stunning results! Several interior designers seeing the value of the bold and beautiful cacti now use them as part of room settings, and you can too. The plants make a striking statement whether used at windows, on tables, or as floor plants in contemporary, modern, or traditional rooms.

By nature, cacti are strong plants that can survive, if necessary, intolerable conditions—think of their desert environments—so this makes them perfect candidates in homes where dry air would kill other plants. If you neglect to water cacti for a few weeks they will not die like a fern or a philodendron. Their fleshy stems contain quantities of water that can tide them over long periods of drought—or your forgetfulness.

In addition, cacti are naturally slow growing and live for years with reasonable care so they are a worthwhile investment. The best-known succulents are members of the family Cactaceae—the cacti—but not all succulents are cacti. This is a group found in many plant families.

While many cacti are splendid decoration as table or desk plants or at windows, larger cacti are impressive room plants appearing like pieces of sculpture. Some might be carved from jade they appear so handsome.

1

Of the 2,000 different cacti, this book contains only a sampling. These are the plants I have used through the years in my home and found to be acceptable under my average home conditions. I hope you will find the plants as rewarding as I do. This is not a technical treatise on the family Cactaceae which is fully covered in many books on the subject. Rather, it is a book for plant lovers who want to use cacti as decorative accents in the home to beautify and delight the eye.

Jack Kramer

1. Versatile Cacti

If you have always thought of cacti as spiny plants of the desert you are in for a surprise. These beautiful and bizarre plants are much more than part of a desert landscape; most make superlative house plants. Hobbyists throughout the country have outstanding collections, but the average person seeking a good house plant rarely thinks of cacti. Yet they are attractive indoor plants and provide dramatic accents.

PLANT SHAPES, COLORS, AND SIZES

The varieties of cacti are almost infinite. Some are shaped like candelabra, others are formed like giant columns, and still others look like globes or barrels. These different shapes provide accent for all areas. For example, in room corners use the large candelabra- or columnar-type cacti such as *Cleistocactus* and *Trichocereus*. Where mass is needed in a room, choose the barrel- or globe-shaped cacti such as the *Mammillaria* or *Lobivia*. Plant colors are as varied as shapes: golden; leather green; and apple green with shades and hues in between—an infinite array of green and gold tones to complement interiors.

There are different sizes of cacti too: small plants for beautiful dish gardens on the table, medium-sized plants for window gardens, and large cacti for living room accent. In addition, if you are fond of flowers, there are Christmas cacti, *Epiphyllums*, and *Rhipsalis*—cacti distinct from their desert cousins because they grow in moist, shady jungles. These plants are ideal for hanging baskets; they provide a cascade of color.

3

CACTI
Plant shape

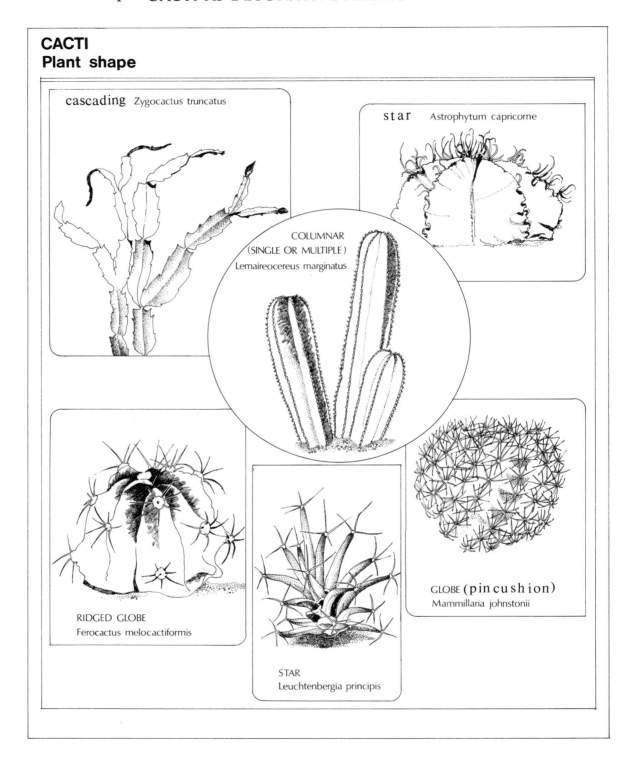

cascading Zygocactus truncatus

star   Astrophytum capricorne

COLUMNAR
(SINGLE OR MULTIPLE)
Lemaireocereus marginatus

RIDGED GLOBE
Ferocactus melocactiformis

STAR
Leuchtenbergia principis

GLOBE (pincushion)
Mammillaria johnstonii

Cacti can be used as decorative accents in many areas of the home; here some small cacti and succulents flank a dramatic Opuntia species. The Opuntia acts as vertical accent, colorful and interesting in the room corner. (*Photo by Max Eckert, Jack Lowrance, Designer*)

WHERE CACTI COME FROM

Most people know that cacti come from deserts, but their concept of a desert is often inaccurate; that is, it is not always a sandy waste-land without any rain. Deserts (in the classification of climates) have an annual rainfall of about 10 inches. Cacti grow from the tip of South America up through the United States to British Columbia in Canada, with perhaps the richest array in Mexico. They are especially abundant in the western deserts of the United States and high in the mountains of Peru, Bolivia, and Argentina. In some of these areas there are heavy rainfalls followed by months of drought. In other areas cacti grow where it rarely rains but where there is a heavy dew or mist frequently. A few cacti even grow under heavy snow in British Columbia.

WHAT ARE CACTI?

Cacti, with few exceptions, are leafless plants with flattened or ribbed bodies, the stems, rather than the leaves as with other plants, manufacturing the food. Most cacti have spines, but not all spines are needlelike; many species bear furry spines soft as velvet. Others, such as *Cephalocereus senilis* (old man cactus) are covered with silky hairs to protect the outside of the plant from drying wind and sun.

Most cacti are succulent plants, but not all succulents are cacti. Succulent plants occur in many plant families, such as the lily. The term succulent applies to plants that have developed water-storage cells in their leaves. Succulent cacti are either epiphytic or desert types. The epiphytes grow in trees in the jungle and have flattened leaflike stems, for example, Christmas cactus and *Rhipsalis*. Desert cacti are more variable in form; they may be columnar- or globe-shaped, large or small. Some cacti have pronounced ribs so the plant can expand and contract as it gains or loses water, and others have tubercles.

CACTI FLOWERS

Cacti flowers, generally short-lived, make up for their brief beauty by producing generally large, brilliant colored blooms in many colors except true blue. The flowers are usually bell-shaped or star-shaped and may vary in size from ⅜ to 7 inches across (for example, *Epiphyllums*). Many cacti flowers open only during the day and close in the evening, lasting a day or two. Some, like *Echinopsis*, open at night, and night-blooming *Cereus* blossom into beauty around midnight and fade by morning. Others, such as *Rebutias* and *Parodias*, bear successive flowers, one opening as another one fades, so a plant may be in bloom several weeks. In any case, you will find that cacti have vividly colored flowers rather than pastel shades.

Some cacti will bloom indoors, if light is sufficient. Some, however, may never attain blooming size because of maturity rather

CACTI
Flower habit

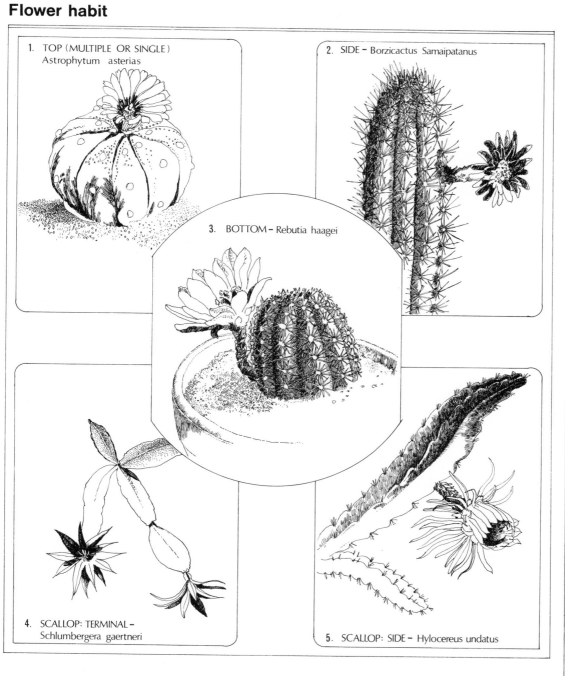

1. TOP (MULTIPLE OR SINGLE)
   Astrophytum asterias

2. SIDE – Borzicactus Samaipatanus

3. BOTTOM – Rebutia haagei

4. SCALLOP: TERMINAL –
   Schlumbergera gaertneri

5. SCALLOP: SIDE – Hylocereus undatus

than light. Yet even without flowers, cacti are splendid accents indoors that require very little care for the amount of beauty they bring to the home.

The following list, which describes the general characteristics of different groups of cacti, will help you determine which plants are best suited for your needs. By choice this is a simplified list and does not include all the numerous groups of plants.

List of Cacti

Astrophytum. Sea urchin cactus, bishop's cap, and goat-horn cactus are in this group. Usually globular shaped or with prominent ribs,

Flowers of the prickly pear cactus (*Opuntia*) are large and colorful and bloom profusely although they last only a day or so. (*USDA photo*)

ASTROPHYTUM ASTERIAS

some have a covering of woolly hair. Flowers are yellow to red. These small plants are excellent indoors at windows or for dish gardens.

Cephalocereus. The familiar old man cactus, *Cephalocereus senilis*, exemplifies this group: tall columnar or branching growth, usually covered by long woolly hair. Most of them flower at night but only rarely indoors. Good as medium-sized accent pot plant for table or desk. Need winter rest and coolness (45°F.).

Cereus. Eventually these cacti make tree-sized plants to 30 feet or more, but young ones are fine house plants. Large (to 8 inches) white flowers on old plants appear at night. Stems are blue-green. Tough plants that grow quickly with little care. For the person who cannot grow anything.

Chamaecereus. Bright flowers in red shades will appear indoors on these small, clump-forming plants. Short shoots branch from the base to produce the clump effect. Plants need a cool winter rest with plenty of sun to bloom indoors.

Cleistocactus. In nature some species grow to 6 feet tall; all are recognizable by a definite narrowing of the stem near the growing point. Stems are usually no more than 1 inch thick, often leaning, and so thickly covered with spines that the stem surface is hardly visible. These are easy to grow, and the orange to red flowers are profuse, and do bloom indoors on mature (5 feet) plants.

Coryphantha. These globular or cylindrical plants (some as much as 12 inches high), with interesting spine patterns, have large yellow, red, or purple flowers. Definite winter rest is required. Grow in porous soil; intolerant of stagnant root conditions.

Echinocactus. Included here are the most familiar barrel-shaped cacti. They are heavily spined and produce flowers from near the crown of mature plants. Young plants are good container subjects; mature specimens may be several feet in diameter.

Cephalocereus is the dominant plant in this corner grouping providing a bold statement against the leafy palms and ferns. (*Photo by Matthew Barr*)

Echinocereus. Usually these are free-branching clusters or mounds of erect stems, sometimes prostrate, and usually less than a foot tall. All have highly ornamental spines that densely cover the plant surfaces. Showy flowers (to 4 inches across) are long-lasting. Need a good porous soil as they do not tolerate soggy soil.

Echinopsis. These small and cylindrical or globular plants have definite vertical ribs. Flowers are long-tubed and many-petaled in shades of white, yellow, pink, or red and may reach 6 to 8 inches in length. *Echinopsis* are among the least demanding cacti as to soil, amount of water, and light.

Epiphyllum. With flattened, scalloped, bright-green leaves (usually pendant) *Epiphyllum*, called orchid cactus, bear large, stunning flowers in an array of colors. Many fine hybrids. A forest plant that needs good air circulation, bright light, and water all year.

Gymnocalycium. The plant bodies are usually globular, with regularly arranged protuberances that give them the name chin cactus. Flowers are red, pink, or white on plants less than 10 inches high. Plants need a rich soil and good moisture; will respond to bright (not sunny) locations.

Lobivia. Small and globular or cylindrically shaped with big, showy flowers in shades of red, yellow, pink, orange, purple, and lilac. Flowers are sometimes nearly as big as the plants. Excellent plants for beginners, *Lobivias* are easy to grow. Give these cacti coolness (65°F.) for best results.

Mammillaria. Small and cylindrically or globe shaped, these plants may be single stemmed or clustered. Red, pink, yellow, or white flowers are usually small, arranged in a circle near the plant's top. Some are easy, fast-growing species, others touchy and hard to

This window garden shows many forms of cacti from tall spires to globes. (*Photo by author*)

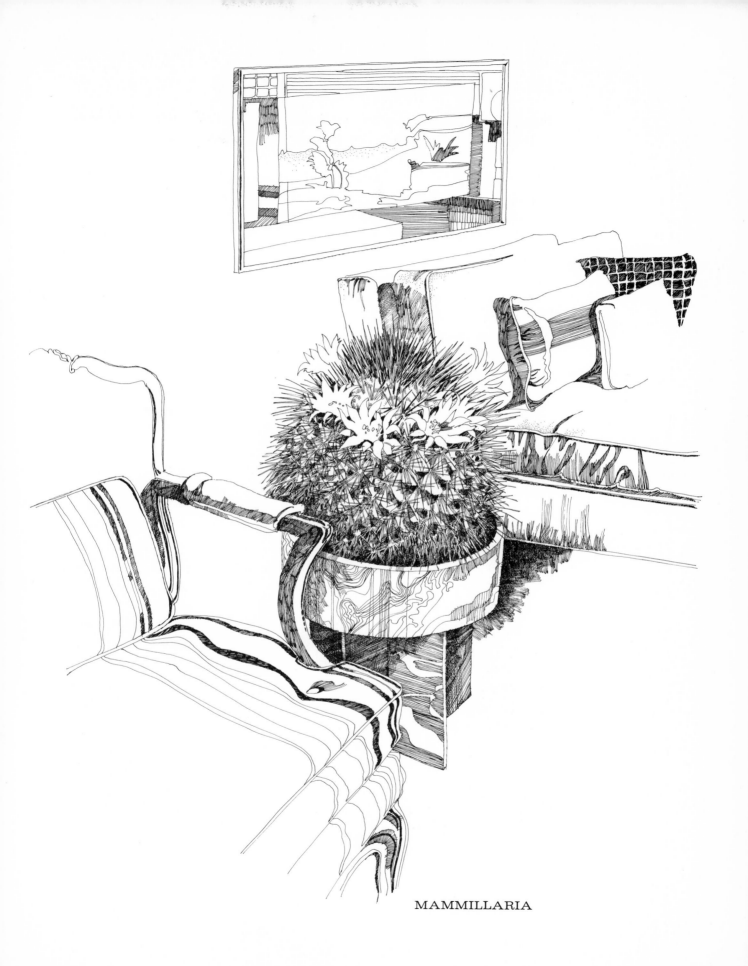

MAMMILLARIA

cultivate. Because there are so many *Mammillarias* it is difficult to give cultural hints. Most like a sandy soil; some a richer soil.

Notocactus. These small ball cacti from South America are easily grown and free flowering. Flowers are yellow or purplish-red. These are vigorous plants, excellent for beginners as they seem to flourish in any situation.

Opuntia. This genus includes the prickly pears, beaver tail, and chollas. Generally it is divided into three groups based upon growth form: the prickly pears, which have flat pads; the tall cylindrical chollas; and the short species, with globe or cylindrically shaped stems. Some make excellent landscape subjects, and others are fine for window gardens. Most are free flowering with white, yellow, orange, purple, or red blooms. *Opuntias* need a rich soil and plenty of water in summer and even in winter don't let them dry out.

Parodia. These small species are similar to *Notocactus*; they flower heavily, have decorative (usually curving) spines, and most species require little attention.

Rebutia. Small and globular species native to high altitudes, *Rebutias* bear flowers from the sides or from around the base; flowers are large for the size of the plant. These plants come from high altitudes so coolness is the key to success here.

Rhipsalis. Rhipsalis are epiphytic, trailing plants that require the same culture as *Epiphyllum* (see Chapter 9). Some species have flattened stems, but the majority have slender cylindrical segments. Flowers are small and not showy. Plants need an airy situation and good moisture at the roots. Grow in equal parts of fir bark and soil for success with them.

A floriferous cactus is *Rhipsalidopsis* "China Pink" with dozens of flowers. It is a medium-sized plant, excellent for windows or in hanging baskets, and requires little care. (*Photo courtesy Johnson Cactus Gardens*)

Rebutias represent the globe or barrel-shaped cacti; this is *Rebutia kessel-ringiana*, a small, lovely plant suitable for any bright location indoors. (*Photo courtesy Johnson Cactus Gardens*)

Schlumbergera. A many-branched cacti, with beautiful purple to scarlet flowers. Sometimes called Christmas cactus. Forest grower.

Thelocactus. These small and globular or cylindrical plants are notable for their especially decorative spines. Flowers are around 2 inches across, red, pink, yellow, or white, and appear at the plant's top.

Zygocactus. This formerly was known as Christmas cactus; leaves resemble lobster claws and bear bright red or pink flowers at leaf tips. A favorite. Forest grower that needs good air circulation and coolness.

This Arizona landscape shows the saguaro cactus (long and vertical), barrel cactus in center and cholla cactus in foreground, a variety of shapes. (*USDA photo*)

2. Cacti as Living Decoration

Versatility determines a good indoor plant, and cacti excel in this category. There are plants for any room in the home, whether it be a dish garden for the table, some plants at a window, or a lovely specimen plant used as a sculptural design in the living area. And, of course, there are collectors' plants too—bizarre but beautiful cacti for the discriminating hobbyist.

From green globes to fingerlike forms to tree types, there are an infinite number of good house plants in the cacti world. And best of all, unlike many house plants that require meticulous care, most cacti can fend for themselves if absolutely necessary. Remember that cacti are plants that can store water in case of drought, so if you are away from your home for a few weeks, cacti will survive whereas other plants like ferns and philodendrons might perish. Because there are so many different kinds of cacti for home decoration, here is an easy classification of plant shapes.

POPULAR PLANT SHAPES

GENERALLY CASCADING

Aporocactus
Epiphyllum
Hylocereus
Rhipsalidopsis
Rhipsalis
Schlumbergera

CLEISTOCACTUS STRAUSII

Selenicereus
Zygocactus

COLUMNAR (SINGLE OR BRANCHED)

Cephalocereus
Cereus
Cleistocactus
Lemaireocereus
Lophocereus
Oreocereus
Pachycereus
Pleistocactus
Trichocereus

GLOBE OR BARREL

Echinocactus
Echinopsis

This window garden of cacti and succulents includes: (left to right) *Aloe arborescens, Mammillaria elongata, Aloe nobilis, Opuntia microdasys, Echinopsis, Euphorbia splendens, Opuntia monacantha, Haworthia* species, *Aloe arborescens* and a small *Hylocereus. (Photo by Jack Roche)*

PARODIA

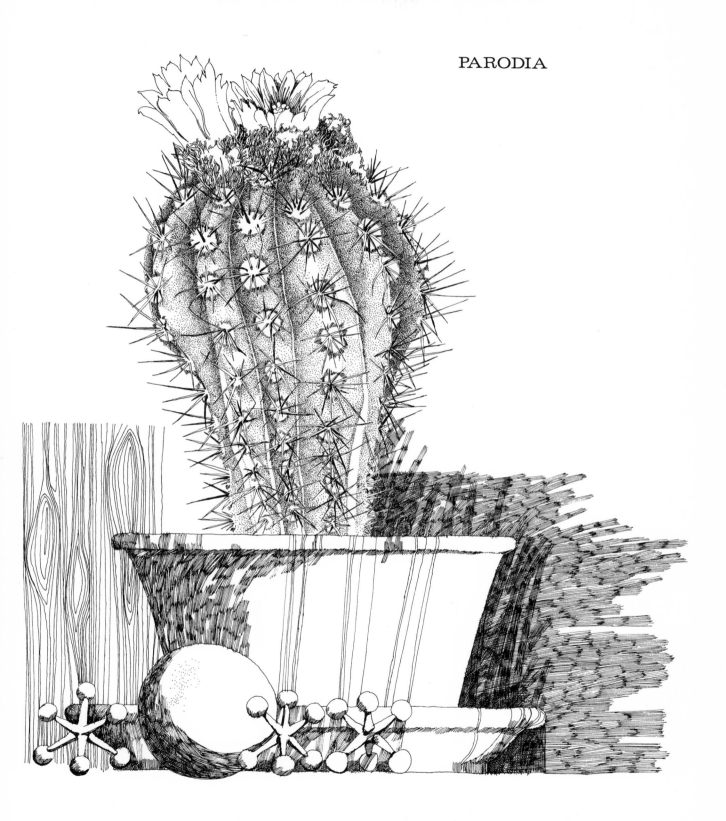

Ferocactus
Frailea
Gymncocalycium
Lobivia
Mammillaria
Notocactus
Parodia
Thelocactus

Star-shaped

Astrophytum
Leuchtenbergia

Window Gardens

Small- and medium-sized cacti are desirable for windows. If grown with reasonable care they never become straggly or unkempt like other house plants, and their forms and shapes make them look like stone carvings silhouetted in morning light or evening dusk. But as with most plant families there are some plants better for window growing than others, so selection along with care is important.

You can put cacti at almost any window, but east or south locations are the best to ensure healthy plants because there they get needed sun and thus prosper. Normal home temperatures will suit most cacti, and as winter approaches and plants enter their rest cycle the temperature will normally drop near windows, which is ideal for cacti.

Just how you arrange your window garden makes a difference. For example, I prefer plants in the same color pots so there is harmony in the overall effect. I also like easy accessibility to the plants so I can watch and water them without trouble. On sills, the problem of water stain must be considered (unless sills are tile), so remember to buy appropriate saucers to catch excess water or use plant trays (sold at nurseries). In either case, a layer of stone pebbles placed in the bottom of the saucer or tray will help to add some humidity to the area as water evaporates on the pebbles.

If you prefer a shelf arrangement at windows, do try to use glass ones so the shelving does not obscure light coming through the

Cleistocactus strausii is the dominant table plant in this photo; the vertical accent with low-growing succulents makes this a handsome setting. (*Photo by Max Eckert*)

window for other plants below. Hardware stores have brackets and attachments to hold glass shelving. Special window greenhouses are also available, if you have a double-hung window; they make excellent display "containers" for cacti.

DESK AND TABLE PLANTS

Plants at windows are fine but cacti can also accent desks and tables where they appear as a decorative accessory. In an ornamental container some of the small- to medium-sized cacti make a fine addition to a room; *Astrophytums* and small *Echinocactus* are excellent candidates for these areas. Try to find really handsome specimens perfect in every detail as these plants are always on display.

In a fireplace corner of the author's home, *Cereus peruvianus monstrosus* appears like a piece of carved jade against a white wall. (*Photo by Matthew Barr*)

The size of the table or desk will of course dictate what size plant to use; in all cases be sure it is in scale with the furnishings. Tiny plants appear out of proportion and large plants smother the setting. Seek the unusual and colorful cactus.

When you have plants on a table or desk be sure to provide adequate protection against water stain on wood. Use a decorative cork mat; on top of this a saucer, then the potted plant. If away from windows, after a few weeks use a different cactus (from the window garden), and return the original choice to better light. This way, plants will not suffer from low light levels and there will be variety in your furniture plants.

Astrophytum asterias. This is a flattened plant with 8 spineless ribs, grayish-green and covered with white spots: pale yellow flowers. Does not bloom until mature.

A. capricorne (goat horn). A green globe with silver markings; 3-inch flowers are yellow with red throats. Resents overwatering so grow on dry side.

A. ornatum. Globular to columnar and ribbed plants; both spines and blooms are yellow.

Cephalocereus palmeri (woolly torch). Hardy plants, with short blue-green spines and tufts of white, woolly hair; columnar to branching growth.

C. senilis (old man cactus). Ribbed columnar growth; spines are hidden in long white hairs.

Chamaecereus. Johnson hybrids (giant peanuts). These resemble a huge peanut; the large flowers range from orange to red.

C. silvestrii (peanut cactus). Dense clusters of short, green branches; red blooms.

Coryphantha poselgeriana. Blue-green, warty-growth clusters and long, stiff spines; large reddish-purple flowers. Needs very porous soil.

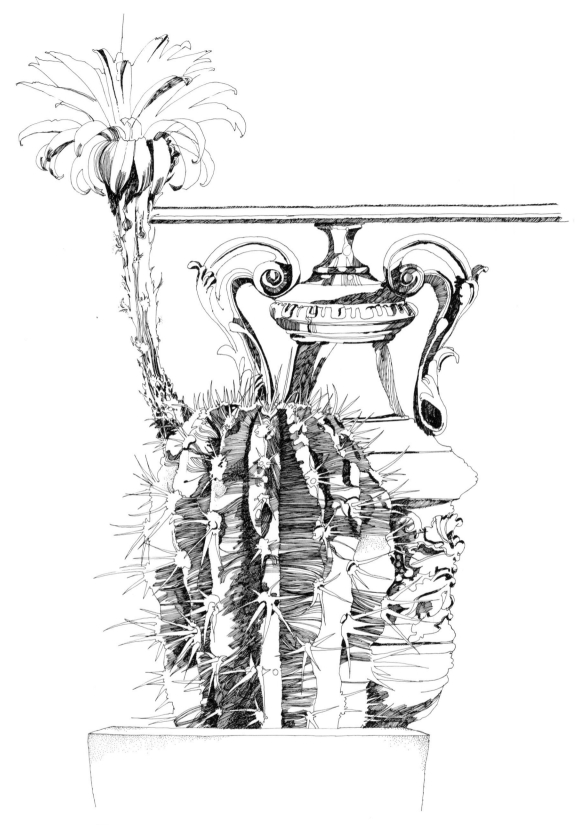

ECHINOPSIS RHODOTRICHA

26

Echinocactus grusonii (golden barrel). Straight and sharp golden spines; with age this plant develops a crown of yellow wool.

E. horizonthalonius. This one grows to about 10 inches in diameter, globular in shape with thick grayish spines. Needs excellent drainage to prosper.

Echinocereus baileyi. Columnar growth, white spines; the open-faced flowers are generally yellow. Keep dry in winter.

E. dasyacanthus (rainbow cactus). Small, columnar plant covered with soft spines; large yellow blossoms. Keep dry in winter.

E. ehrenbergii. Erect stems, free branching from base, with slender, glassy white spines; purple-red flowers. Keep dry in winter.

E. reichenbachii (lace cactus). Small, heavily spined plant with red and yellow flowers.

Echinopsis multiplex. A thick-spined plant with very pale pink flowers. The Johnson *Echinopsis* hybrids are outstanding and the best of this group, I believe.

A group of fine, small, window cacti unique in shape and texture. (*USDA photo*)

E. rhodrotricna. Spiny, stout, ribbed column. Can grow large.

Gymnocalycium bruchii. One of the small clump-forming species with short spines. Flowers are white, tinged pink. Easy growing.

G. mihanovichii. A ribbed cacti, grayish green and sometimes with reddish markings. Plant grows to about 2 inches and bears pink or yellowish flowers with little care.

Lobivia haageana. One of the most attractive *Lobivias* with a ribbed body and about 12 inches tall and 4 inches in diameter. Flowers are pale yellow. Blooms when young.

L. hertrichiana. A small plant, ribbed and bright green. Flowers are fiery red, produced in quantity and plants bloom when young.

Mammillaria bocasana (powder puff cactus). Clustering growth and hooked central spine covered with white hair; small yellow flowers.

M. celsiana. A flattened globular plant somewhat depressed at the crown and covered with spines. This cactus bears small red flowers with little care.

Notocactus mammulosus (lemon ball). A globular and ribbed plant, gray to brown in color with short spines; yellow flowers. Easy to grow, but don't overwater.

N. scopa (silver ball). Globular, ribbed, and covered with soft, white spines; yellow flowers. Don't overwater.

Opuntia basilaris (beaver tail). Upright blue-green growths from compact pads; withstands low temperatures. Blooms range from pink to carmine.

Tall and stately, this *Trichocereus* species makes a bold statement in a dining room corner; it is massive and dramatic and furnishes needed vertical accent. (*Photo by Matthew Barr*)
Flanked by french doors a candelabra *Cereus* cactus decorates this setting. (*Photo by Matthew Barr*)

CEREUS CACTUS

BORZICACTUS

31

Parodia aureispina (Tom Thumb cactus). Small globular plant with golden spines; golden flowers. Easier to grow than most *Parodias*.

P. sanguiniflora. A globular, small white-spined species; red flowers. Keep evenly moist except in winter when dry rest is needed.

Rebutia minuscula (red clown). Clustering globular plants of green heads; large brick-red flowers. Needs coolness to thrive.

Rhipsalis paradoxa. Epiphytic. Flat green leaves with sawtooth edges; tiny white flowers. Grow in mixture of osmunda and soil; keep moist all year.

FLOOR PLANTS

For our purposes a floor plant is defined as specimen size: large (sometimes to 7 feet) and at the peak of beauty. Such plants are rarely inexpensive, but like a piece of furniture they will be with you for years with proper care. Their sculptural growth patterns and shapes and striking colors make specimen cacti unbeatable indoor accents. The upright- and tree-type cacti are especially effective against light colored walls because of their beautiful silhouettes. When placed in suitable ornamental containers tall cacti are like sculptures and add drama to a room.

Some cacti, for example *Lemaireocereus thurberi*, have a candelabra growth habit, with great spires piercing the sky; they are indeed dramatic in any room, whether contemporary or period. *Trichocereus spachianus*, brilliant green and sculptural in form, is another fine showpiece for a room. Some of the *Echinocacti* are round, beautiful globes of green laced with golden spines and provide a glowing spot of color indoors.

Not every room is right for large cacti. As mentioned, the plants make a bold statement and thus must be used as a design element rather than just another house plant. However, where suitable, cacti have no peer in the plant world.

Here is a sampling of large cacti for floor plants. Species names are confusing as taxonomical changes are made periodically. We have tried to include the most recent names.

OPUNTIA

Borzicactus. A genus name that covers several genera; generally slender branching plants, columnar or prostrate with beautifully colored spines.

Carnegia gigantea. Handsome curving branches; angular and vertical.

Cephalocereus. Many different species; now known as *Pilocereus.* Generally branching tall plants. *C. dybowski* is erect and slender to 12 feet, cylindrical and covered with white wool.

Cereus hildmannianus. Very tall, branching and columnar. Stunning room accent.

C. peruvianus. Treelike and big and massive. *C. peruvianus monstrosus* ribbed and somewhat contorted; dark green. Unique accent.

Cleistocactus strausii. Erect plant; bold and big.

Echinocactus grusonii (golden barrel). Can grow 4 feet around with golden spines; makes a bold statement. Use low tubs.

Euphorbia lactea. Not a cactus but close enough. This one has angular contorted ribs, green-brown with spines.

Furcraea gigantea. Rosette of shiny green; narrow spiny leaves to 7 inches.

Lemaireocereus marginatus. Treelike and sculptural; small stiff spines. Easy to grow.

L. thurberi. A ribbed columnar giant, branching and growing to great heights. Purplish-green with black spines.

Lophocereus schotti. A 5- to 7-ribbed apple green giant; branching with short spines. Likes warmth.

Opuntia basilaris. Oval pads of soft green; nearly spineless. Fine

TRICHOCEREREUS GLOTTSBERGII

rugged accent for contemporary rooms. Several species suitable as room accents.

Trichocereus glottsbergii. Columnar; small and stout; prominent spines.

T. spachianus. Strong, short columnar growth; short spines and white flowers. Easy to grow.

For dish garden plants, see Chapter 4; for hanging plants and plants under lights, see Chapter 3.

3. Cacti as Special Accents

Besides being used as floor and window plants, there are other ways that cacti provide unique decorative notes indoors; they are especially rewarding as hobbyist plants under artificial light or as specimen plants with display lighting. (Gardening under light has many advantages for the indoor gardener and increases daily in popularity.)

Cascades of green in hanging containers are also part of the cacti and succulent garden decor. Many species make beautiful accents at eye level and indeed in suitable containers are just as popular as ferns or vines. In terrariums, the smaller cacti can bring a desert setting to your desk or coffee table. When well planted the desert terrarium is a lovely scene that complements any interior.

ARTIFICIAL LIGHT

Under fluorescent or incandescent light, plants have no rest because there is constant "sunshine." Culture too is somewhat different than growing plants at windows, and temperature, humidity, and a good circulation of air necessary to keep cacti at their peak. Although it is essential that plants have good humidity, be sure they do not have too much moisture in the air or rot may develop. Water plants under lights every other day in spring and summer when growth is at its peak. In fall and winter, water twice a week. Be sure the growing unit is in a place where there is a good circulation of air because few plants thrive in stagnant air conditions. Keep plants 3 to 4 inches from the light source. Smaller cacti pots can be placed on inverted clay pots or bricks, and the larger ones can stay in the tray furnished with the unit. Keep light on for 12 to 14 hours a day.

In addition to promoting the growth of smaller plants in hobby carts, artificial light can also sustain large floor plants in good health for many months. Under suitable lamps plants benefit from the light and at the same time are uniquely silhouetted, adding to the beauty of a room.

FLUORESCENT. Commercially made small carts and table models are available in many sizes from suppliers. These units come equipped with fluorescent tubes and adjustable shelves. For the gardener who loves live plants at home but does not have natural light this is an ideal answer. There are also special Grow-lamps sold under various trade names for plants. Generally the smaller cacti are best grown in light trays and carts. Usually these plants do bloom, at which point they can be moved to appropriate places where you can enjoy the flowers.

INCANDESCENT. Frequently, plants are in shady corners where light is minimal. Fluorescent light is used mainly by hobbyists for cart and tray growing, but there are not yet enough suitable and attractive fixtures for these lamps for living room decor. Thus, use incandescent

A good trailing cactus is *Aporophyllum* "Star Fire" with brilliant red blooms on scandent stems. Plants are large and awkward but flowers beautiful and impressive when grown in hanging baskets. (*Photo by author*)
Artificial light stands are available in many models. This floor cart with fluorescent lights accommodates many plants, some cacti on top row. (*Photo courtesy Burpee Seed Co.*)

light, which can supply most of the vital light rays a plant needs. Manufacturers offer an array of esthetically pleasing fixtures that match almost any decor.

The lamps and fixtures can be used on walls or in a light track (strip of hardware) on ceilings. Can- or bullet-type fixtures are then placed on the light strip. All that is needed to maintain plant growth is one or two 250-watt incandescent lamps aimed (flood type) at the plant. The lamps will have to be on 12 to 14 hours a day, so do install a separate circuit for them. Cost is somewhat high, about

This hanging plant is a *Rhipsalis* hybrid; it is perfect for a hanging container where it receives bright light and good air circulation. (*Photo by Matthew Barr*)

$60.00 for installation, but specimen cacti are expensive, so it's worth the additional cost to keep plants in good health and to ensure that they will live for years.

Almost any small or medium-size cactus can be grown under lights with good results. Indeed with *Lobivas*, *Parodias*, and *Rebutias* you will have an abundance of flowers. Larger cacti (referred to as floor plants in this book) are of course too large for cart growing but can be used as display plants with proper flood lamp installations.

CASCADING PLANTS

Most plant families have some species that are suitable for hanging baskets. Several cacti and succulents can be grown in this manner. They make handsome plants with their cascading leaves and can be used indoors or out as superb decorative accents. For a real display group several plants of the same species together. The beauty of baskets is when they are brimming full.

Plants at eye level in hanging containers are popular because they are easily seen from all sides and because with air circulation around the container grow better. Many cacti, natural tree dwellers, are especially well suited to basket culture. *Aporocactus* are excellent subjects with bright foliage and flowers. In an airy situation with good light they respond beautifully. So do *Epiphyllums*, the popular orchid-cacti. *Schlumbergeras* and *Zygocactus* known as Easter and Christmas cacti become a halo of color in baskets. (See Chapter 9.) *Rhipsalis* species are other gems that offer cascading color in the air.

Prepare the container with care for basket growing. Open wire baskets are fine; these should be lined with sphagnum moss and then filled with equal parts of osmunda and soil. If you have wood floors and water stain presents a problem, use clay pots with saucers attached to catch excess water. (Moss liners are not needed in these pots.) With basket plants, remember to water them well throughout the year; they are forest dwellers and not desert cacti. Most will do fine with a bright location rather than intense sun.

Sedum morganianum, known as the donkey's tail, is a familiar succulent plant. The leaves are apple green and can cascade to 5 feet or more. (*Photo by Hort-Pix*)

It may take several years for the cascading cacti to really be beautiful but once established they are a stunning sight.

Here are some favorite basket cacti and succulents:

Aporocactus. In their native lands (Central America and Mexico) these plants hang from trees or rocks. The best known member of the group is *A. flagelliformis*, known as the rat-tail cactus. Don't let the name deter you; it is a handsome plant with slender stems, ribbed, and densely covered with brownish spines. The tubular flowers are about 2 inches across and bloom in spring, making quite a display. Grows readily in average room conditions.

Rhipsalis. These plants resemble the slender *Epiphyllums*; they have angular or flat leaflike stems with many joints, small flowers, and bear white berries that make them most attractive. To be at their best they must really be full and lush or else they look scrawny. Pendant stems can grow to 5 feet.

Schlumbergera. These Easter cactus are now relegated to the genus *Rhipsalidopsis*. These fascinating floriferous plants are excellent for basket growing because they become a halo of green, with a crown of bright flowers. There are several hybrids; you will generally find them at florists at seasonal times. The Christmas cactus is also in this group but will probably always be found under its former name, *Zygocactus truncatus*.

Selenicerous. These are the plants known as "Queen of the Night." The plants have long, trailing, awkward gray green stems with brown spines. The flowers are mammoth, some to 12 inches. *S. Macdonaldiae* and *S. grandiflorus* are usually seen.

Sedums. These are succulents and included here because they grow with little care. In a short time they can completely cover a container and become a spectacular sight. My favorites include *S. Sieboldii*, a natural creeper with notched blue-gray leaves edged red; and *S. morganianum* (donkey's tail), extremely popular, with spindle-shaped yellow-green foliage on long pendulous stems. Also pretty is *S. stahlii* (coral beads); this plant has a spreading habit with dark green to brown foliage.

Appearing as a natural desert scene this terrarium has several small cacti. The enclosure is not completely sealed; air slots are provided at the base and in between glass sections. (*Photo by author*)

This small *Opuntia* is charming in a stained-glass wall terrarium. Top opens to provide adequate ventilation. (*Design by Richard Lee; photo by Matthew Barr*)

TERRARIUMS

This popular kind of gardening deserves mention because it creates a pleasing scene—a lilliputian world where you can delight in nature. The terrarium may be glass or plastic, large or small, but always be sure the opening is large enough to accommodate small barrel- and globe-shaped cacti. What you are trying to do behind the glass is create a diminutive nature scene; this is easily done. However, in terrariums there are no drainage holes, so a different set of planting rules is necessary.

Select a pleasing container—a wide-mouth decanter, a goldfish bowl, or any attractive transparent container. Put in a 1-inch bed of gravel to help excess moisture evaporate that might otherwise sink to the bottom of the terrarium. On top of the gravel scatter a thin layer of charcoal to keep the soil sweet. For a soil base use a rich house-plant mixture; pour in 3 or 4 inches. Now plan the garden. Make hills and valleys rather than an uninteresting flat terrain. Put in thin layers of stone to simulate rock outcroppings and perhaps some colored gravel here and there for contrast.

Buy seedlings in 2- or 3-inch pots, and move them around in the terrarium until you find a pleasing arrangement. Now gently remove plants from their pots, and place them in pre-dug holes. Put tall plants in the rear and smaller plants in front and at the sides. Leave the center of the terrarium open for viewing. Firm the soil around the collar of the cacti; do not plant them too deeply or they may rot. Set the glass garden in a bright but not sunny place and enjoy nature.

Use care when watering the terrarium; too much moisture can cause rot, and not enough water will starve plants. Try to keep an evenly moist soil. Do not feed plants because you want them to stay small in your miniature scene. For a discussion of terrarium plants see the next chapter (any dish garden plant can be used).

4. Dish Gardens

Window plants are charming, and floor plants add drama to any room, but dish gardens—a group of cacti—have a place in the home too. They provide a bright interest on tables, desks, and interior locations. But the dish garden planted haphazardly is an eyesore; just *how* the miniature garden is planted and *in what* constitutes its success. You must have compatible plants (not all cacti like the same conditions), drainage, and the right amounts of watering, light, and temperature.

Planning the Garden

If possible, make your own dish gardens; it is easy and fun, and they will be better (even the amateur attempts) than purchased ones, which are often quickly planted with any plant that is on hand. Use both small and large plants, and strive for balance and harmony. The container can be of any size but be sure it is at least 4 inches deep so plants have a good base of soil to grow in. Try to create a miniature replica of the desert in nature. A flat design with a level grading is dull and monotonous; use hills and valleys and provide some small rocks for dimension. Make the front low, and mound the soil somewhat in the rear. Place rock outcroppings (shale is excellent). There are many variations; use your imagination. Before you start the dish garden, place the potted plants in the container, and move them around until you find the right placement, a scene that is pleasing to the eye. If you buy plants in 2- or 3-inch containers— and you should—this is an easy procedure. Set the largest plant to one side of the dish, never in the center. Create an arc with small plants around the larger one.

Dish garden components: soil, gravel, plants and shallow container. Note stones at bottom of container for drainage. (*Photo by Matthew Barr*)

Starting the dish garden with vertical stones and a small upright cactus. (*Photo by Matthew Barr*)

Round, vertical and rosette plants are used for the garden. (*Photo by Matthew Barr*)

The completed dish garden. (*Photo by Matthew Barr*)

Also consider color: dark green, apple green, or gray-green. Paint the scene as though it were a picture so that all aspects will be attractive.

Planting the Garden

Today, many containers for dish gardens have drainage holes, so plants will grow better in them. However, an old container without holes is also satisfactory, but remember that you will have to water plants in it carefully. As mentioned, the container can be almost any shape or size, but try to select one that is simple in design and outside ornamentation rather than a container that will detract from the plants. Glazed containers (in various colors) will not have drainage holes; bonsai-type dishes are excellent and have drainage holes. Also look for a tapered terra cotta pot, which makes a fine housing for dish gardens because soil dries quickly, so overwatering of plants is less likely to occur.

Prepare the soil for the dish garden carefully You do not want a sandy soil or a heavy garden soil. In the former case the water will drain to the bottom too quickly and not provide plants with enough moisture; in the latter case the water may stagnate at the bottom. Use an equal mixture of garden soil, sand, and gravel or other porous stone.

In a container without holes first put in a layer of stones; this will distribute the water throughout the surface of the bottom rather

This dish garden was made in a glass salad bowl; it includes several small cacti; stones and gravel are on the surface. A garden like this can live for years before replanting is necessary. (*Photo by author*)

A small dish garden of cactus and succulents is used as a centerpiece for a table setting. Plants need little care in shallow dishes and last for years. (*Photo by Jack Roche*)

than let it remain in the soil. Over the gravel sprinkle some chipped charcoal (sold at suppliers). Now add the soil mixture to within ½ inch of the top of the dish. Remove plants by tapping the side of the pot against a table edge and then teasing the plant from the container with as much of the root ball intact as possible. Dig small pockets into the soil and place plants. Do not bury them too deeply or crown rot may occur. Put them in place in the dish at the same level as they were in the pots you bought them. Firm the soil around the collar of the plant to eliminate air pockets in the soil. With dishes that have drainage holes the procedure is the same except that you can eliminate the charcoal; place small pieces of shards (broken parts of clay pots) over the drainage holes so soil and gravel will not fall out.

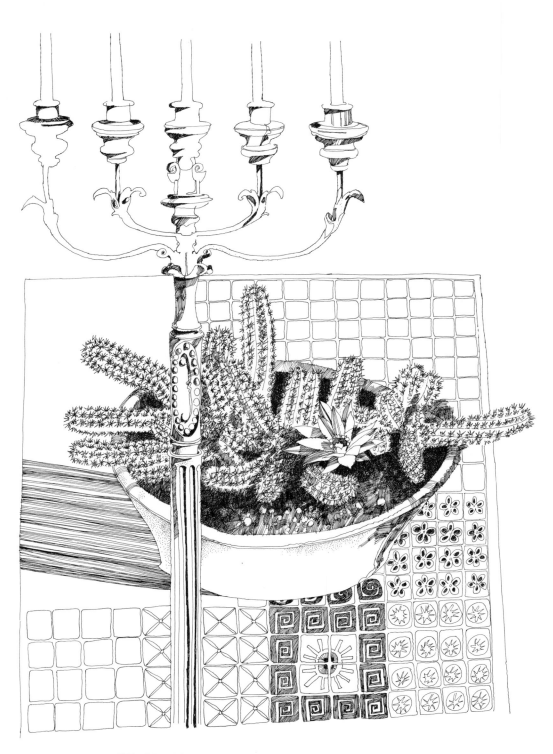

CHAMAECEREUS SILVESTRII

When the dish garden is completed, water it thoroughly and then set in bright light for a few days. After that, put it in a sunny place. Use appropriate clay saucers or mats to protect table surfaces from water stain.

CARE

With dish gardens success depends upon proper watering. Too much water will drown plants and cause soft growth, and too little will result in spindly growth. It is impossible to dictate exact amounts of water for gardens because bowls vary in size and depth, but generally it is always better to give a reasonable amount of water once a week rather than sparse moisture every few days. Scanty watering keeps the surface of the soil wet, but plant roots simply do not get it. All the soil should be evenly moist (after awhile you will be able to judge just how much water your dish garden needs).

When you water plants do not dump water in the dish because it will splash the plants, which is not a good practice. Use a watering can with a thin spout. Tap water is fine, but do not use icy cold water because that shocks plants; let the water stand overnight so it is at room temperature. Water can be applied quite freely during spring and summer, but in fall taper off moisture—perhaps once every 10 days—and in winter give just enough water to keep the soil from caking. Most cacti (not all) need dry conditions from November to March.

All plants, including cacti, need light for healthy growth. Indeed, cacti will require at least a few hours of daily sun to prosper. A south, or east exposure is ideal. West windows will give just enough light for cacti to sustain themselves, but they will grow little, and for dish gardens north light should rarely be used. Be sure too that plants are in an area of good air circulation. Avoid a closed stagnant atmosphere. Ordinary house temperatures are fine for your dish garden plants. A natural drop in temperature at night of about 10 degrees is fine.

Feeding of plants in dish gardens should be done with a light hand, if at all. Use a weak solution of a 5-10-10 fertilizer applied only in summer, about every third week, and not at all the rest of the year. When plants become large (after about 2 years) they will crowd each other. At this point remover the bigger ones and pot

LEUCHTENBERGIA PRINCIPIS

them as single specimens. Remove the plants gently from the bowl, and do a general replanting.

List of Dish Garden Plants

Adromischus maculatus (calico hearts). Gray-green, thick, flat leaves spotted brown; flowers tipped red-white.

Astrophytum myriostigma (bishop's cap). Gray and ribbed spineless oddity; yellow flowers.

Cephalocereus palmeri (woolly torch). Hardy plant. Short blue-green spines and tufts of white, woolly hair; columnar to branching.

Chamaecereus silvestrii (peanut cactus). Dense clusters of short, green branches; red blooms.

Echinocereus melanocentrus. Small, spiny, dark green globe; large red flowers.

Echinopsis kermesiana. Round plant with ribs; lilylike red blooms.

Facucaria tigrina (tiger's jaws). Gray-green leaves with slender teeth, flecked with white; yellow flowers.

Gasteria lilliputana. Mottled dark green and pale green leaves, spirally arranged.

Leuchtenbargia principis. A bizarre but handsome cactus, resembles an *Agave.*

Parodia aureispina (Tom Thumb cactus). Golden spines on a blue-green globe; golden flowers.

Rebutia kupperiana. Small gray globe; free blooming, with red flowers.

R. minuscula. Bright green globe with brick-red blooms.

The following plants are some compatible groupings for dish gardens. The plants have been chosen because of scale, good color, and ease of growing.

Group One:
Astrophytum myriostigma
Maihuenia poeppigi
Opuntia microdasys
Pachycereus pringlei
Rebutia minuscula

GYMNOCALYCIUM DAMSII

GROUP TWO:
Cephalocereus palmeri
Faucaria tigrina
Monanthes polyphylla
Notocactus ottonis

GROUP THREE:
Chamaecereus silvestrii
Notocactus haselbergii
Pachycereus pringlei
Parodia aureispina
Rebutia kupperiana

5. Shopping for Plants

There is more to buying cacti than just choosing this one or that one. Each cacti has a character, a feeling, to make it suitable for specific places in the home. So first determine just where the plant is to be, and then select accordingly. For example, in living rooms you want a large statuesque cacti; for window gardens smaller globe-or barrel-shaped cacti are suitable. Remember that cacti come in a variety of shapes and sizes, so buy intelligently rather than haphazardly.

Where to get cacti deserves some consideration too, and how to get them from shop to home or by mail is fully covered in this section. You also will need some knowledge about containers, of which there are hundreds to choose from. How to handle the cacti (they are spiny) is discussed in the next chapter, in the potting and repotting section.

Where to Get Plants
For small plants, your local Woolworths (or equivalent store) is a good place to start because plants are inexpensive and the stores have a large selection. However, not all plants will be labeled, and if labeled they may be incorrectly named. Even so, this is a good place to shop.

Local florists will have large plants, but they are generally very expensive. Most florists sell gift plants, which means that plants are in peak form but are also at peak prices. Also, selection is limited, so even though you can occasionally find a winner, in most cases you will have to take what you can.

Patio shops and nurseries throughout the country have cacti; these

Small cacti are available at nurseries or Woolworth-type stores. Each carries a label (although not always correctly identified). Here are several species including *Trichocereus, Notocactus, Mammillaria, Cephalocereus* and others. (*Photo by Matthew Barr*)

places generally have an excellent selection of large or small plants. In their greenhouses you may find some beautiful overlooked specimens among other plants, so poke around if you can. Cacti have been overlooked so long by buyers that they are not always prominently displayed. Often I have found beautiful plants hidden away in large greenhouses. For example, two of my finds were a rare *Selenicereus* and a mature *Hylocereus* that today, 15 years later, still bears mammoth flowers once a year.

You can also buy cacti through mail-order companies. There are dozens of these excellent sources (see end of book). Remember when ordering from mail-order companies to select plants by *botanical* name; unless you know what you want by name you might very well get something you do not want. Of course, you can always ask by letter for a specific type of plant (for living room, for window, and so forth), but generally it is much easier just to know the name and get the proper plant.

Do not be afraid to order large plants for shipment from mail-order suppliers; they pack plants carefully and ship them to any destination. Once you receive plants unpack them immediately

Identification of cacti is sometimes a problem but conservatories in cities or college greenhouses generally have some cacti display. These plants were photographed at the University of California in Berkeley, California, and as shown have correct identification with labels intact. (*Photo by Matthew Barr*)

Generally, plants come in plastic starter pots as shown. Repot them when you get them home so they will have fresh soil. (*Photo by Matthew Barr*)

Containers for plants come in all sizes and shapes. Here are examples of decorative pots that add a great deal of beauty to the total setting. Plants in rear are *Aloes*, those in front cacti. (*Photo USDA*)

because the quicker they get in their new conditions the sooner they will provide beauty for your home. Always inspect new plants for disease (mold, fungus, or soft growth) and for insects before you put them in their permanent place. I have an isolation area where new plants are kept a few days before they are assigned permanent places. (If plants are inferior and have disease or insects, take necessary precautions and advise supplier immediately.)

Order plants in spring or fall. In summer, boxes become overheated and plants may be harmed; in winter there is, of course, al-

ways the possibility of plants freezing from cold weather. Have plants shipped air freight collect, if possible, which means overnight delivery in most cases or at least second-day delivery in far-off areas. Check with your local air freight office to determine weights and cost. From Chicago to California the freight rate is $20.00 whether you have 10 or 100 pounds shipped, so air freight is best for large shipments rather than only a few plants. Air Parcel Post is less expensive and acceptable; plants arrive in about a week. Shipping by Greyhound bus is good too. It is inexpensive, but you will have to pick up plants at the local stations.

Specimen plants, that is, plants at peak form, are also available from plant suppliers in large cities such as New York (Terrestris) and Chicago (The Greenhouse). They can be purchased outright or may be rented by the month. Maintenance too is available for a fee.

Containers for Plants

Years ago we were limited to terra cotta pots, but today there are hundreds of different types of containers. The clay pot is still with us in many shapes and sizes, but there are also glazed, plastic, wooden and metal pots. For most cacti I use terra cotta pots because plants grow well in them and there are some lovely shapes made, in particular the Spanish design with outward sloping sides, flared lips, and the perfectly cylindrical pot. Plastic pots are lightweight, which is a disadvantage for cacti because many are heavy and in plastic the plants tend to tip over. Occasionally I do use a glazed container when I want a choice of color or a decorative motif. Most do not have drainage holes, so I take the containers to a local glass store and have holes drilled. Because waterlogged soil has killed too many of my plants through the years I find it is worth the extra effort to have holes drilled. Of course, if breakage occurs in the process, it is your responsibility, not the local workman's.

Some plants look good in wooden tubs, but to my eye cacti rarely are pleasing in them. Metal containers are rarely a good investment because metal deteriorates quickly from soil and constant watering.

Clay pots while not as decorative as ornamental jardinieres and tubs make excellent containers for cacti. They keep roots cool and hold moisture a short time compared to plastic pots, which retain moisture. (*Photo by Matthew Barr*)

Glazed Japanese pots are extremely pretty and cacti look good in them, but they are expensive. Still, for a special place the ornamental Japanese pot is fine. Decorative stone containers are satisfactory housings too but are heavy. But plants grow well in them so you may want to consider using them.

Natural containers, that is, pieces of wood and rock, can also be used as a housing for cacti. Plants look different on them; this is a unique and lovely way to grow small specimens. Choose rocks that have eroded pockets; not every one you find will be suitable for planting. Brush and wash all rock and wood pieces before putting plants on them. In most cases you will have to wire the plants to natural containers until they take hold. Place the plant against the wood or stone in the desired position. Push as much of the root system as you can into the soil. Then wire the plant to the host. It takes about 6 months to a year before plants are permanent; at that point you can remove the wires.

Now a word about the many self-watering containers available. These are a boon for most gardeners, but they are not suitable for all plants; generally cacti do not do well in them. The containers themselves are plastic and lightweight, so tipping of the plant is always a danger. Furthermore, most self-watering containers are not available in very large sizes; for large indoor cacti really big pots are necessary.

6. Care of Plants

Light, watering, and proper soil, and potting and repotting are all essential requirements of cacti. Certain techniques and processes can save you a lot of time and bother; that is what this chapter is all about: general care and some health hints for your plants.

SOIL AND SOIL MIXTURES

Cacti do not grow in pure sand as most people think. Indeed, like other plants they need a good soil mix with the right nutrients to prosper. There are many soil mixtures; just what you choose depends upon whether you are growing small or large plants and the plant itself. Most cacti are desert dwellers, but some, like Christmas cactus, are from the rain forests and thus require different soil.

For most cacti a mix of equal parts of garden loam, sand, and small pebbles is fine. For jungle cacti, for example, *Rhipsalis*, *Schlumbergera*, and *Zygocactus*, you will need a mixture of one part shredded tree bark or osmunda (sold at nurseries) and one part garden loam. The ingredients must be thoroughly mixed and have a friable texture so the medium drains water but yet retains moisture for plant roots.

Prepared soil bought by the bushel from local greenhouses has all the necessary nutrients for plant growth. (I add a little sand and some pebbles to it.) It will be sterilized, so there is little chance for weeds to grow or for bacterial diseases to get started. Packaged soil prepared especially for cacti is also satisfactory, but do avoid packaged mixes specifically marked for African violets or just marked "house plants" because they are generally too heavy and dense for good cacti growth.

Most cacti in their native habitat grow in rocky arid regions indicating their need for a somewhat sandy soil. (*USDA photos*)

Soilless mixes or peat mixes (also available at nurseries), although lightweight and good for some plants, are not suitable for cacti because they contain no nutrients; a careful feeding program must be followed.

LIGHT AND TEMPERATURE

Light is essential to all plant life. Cacti generally do need good light, at least some sun a few hours a day to really thrive. However, even in lesser situations they will still survive if not grow rapidly. Quite frankly, do not expect every cacti to bloom unless they are in a very sunny position. Most will, but others will not. If you want flowers, choose *Zygocactus, Rhipsalis, Lobivias, Parodias, Rebutias*, and *Epiphyllums*. They can, if necessary, produce flowers in lesser light levels. Artificial lighting is discussed in Chapter 3.

Turn plants occasionally (unless they are in bud), so that light reaches all parts of the plant evenly. Otherwise, plants will lean toward the light, and a lopsided cactus is not what you want as a decorative accent.

Some house plants require exacting temperatures, but most cacti are flexible as to temperature and can tolerate anything from 55° to 90°F. without harm. Of course, the optimum is 75°F. by day and

This *Agave* growing outdoors shows the type of soil many succulents and cacti prefer: sandy and somewhat gravelly but with adequate nutrients. (*Photo by author*)

Crassula argentea, the Jade Plant, is a popular succulent and grows well indoors. This plant has done splendidly but after three years needs a new pot. A deeper and wider container is necessary. (*Photo by Joyce R. Wilson*)

65°F. at night. In winter, lower temperatures of say 65°F. by day are very beneficial because most cacti rest in winter and need less warmth.

POTTING AND REPOTTING

Potting cacti is troublesome unless you know a few tricks. Some cacti have spines and others do not, but when repotting plants wear leather gloves. The potting procedure itself is quite simple: Set a large piece of crock over the drainage hole, and put in soil (remember to have stones in it) to about 2 or 4 inches. Mound the soil in the pot, and set the plant in place. If it is too high, take out some soil; if it is too low and the crown of the plant is below the rim of the pot, add soil. Fill in and around the roots with more soil and fill the container. Then settle the soil by rapping the bottom of the pot on a hard surface. Now add a scant covering of pebbles on top so the base of the plant is not in contact with the potting soil. Water sparingly for the first few days so broken roots can heal; they might otherwise rot from excessive moisture.

Do not let spines be a hazard when potting plants. Use a pair of heavy work gloves, a folded newspaper, wooden or metal tongs for handling cacti. Use newspaper or cardboard chute to fill around the plant with soil. This keeps hands far enough away from spines and eliminates pricking or scratching. To make the paper or cardboard chute place soil on a square (at least 12 inches square), and grasp paper from center of opposite sides. This forms a chute; soil will easily fall into place around the plant.

Repotting is removing a plant from an old container and starting it into growth in a new, generally larger, one. This operation is best done in spring or fall. In spring, warm weather is on the way, so plants have a good chance to get started growing, and in fall, weather is still warm, so plants have a chance to adjust before very cold weather sets in.

Large floor plants in containers over 16 inches can go without repotting for 4 years, but eventually they must have new soil with new nutrients. Smaller plants need attention every second year. Repotting a large cactus takes two people. What you want to do is remove the plant without shocking it too much. Let the soil dry somewhat before repotting. Have one person hold the container in

1. shards over hole, 1″ gravel

2. mound of soil

3. cactus in newspaper roll, insert in pot

4. fill in soil using funnel-press down with narrow stick to firm soil

How to Pot a Small Cactus

place as you jiggle the plant slightly to loosen it. Do not rip it from its container; tease it out if at all possible. Once the plant is out of the pot, remove some of the old soil from the roots and then repot as outlined.

Occasionally removing a plant from a large tub or pot becomes a tug-of-war, with you the loser. If this happens, you have two alternatives. If the pot is somewhat soiled and unsightly, break it; it is better to lose a container than a 10-year-old plant. If a plant will not come out of a still-usable container, dig out as much of the soil as possible—at least 4 to 5 inches—and replenish with fresh soil. Special techniques are needed with very large cacti because plants may be awkward and too heavy to handle. For large plants, make a hammock from burlap and lift plants by the burlap, or place large plants on slabs of plywood and move the plywood rather than the plant itself. Have one person hold the plant steady in the pot while the other person does the actual repotting. Even so, once potted some cacti may be too heavy. If so, insert wood props to hold the plant in place.

WATERING

Watering cacti depends on the plant itself, the container, and the kind of soil used. Generally water desert cacti in large containers (over 14 inches) twice a week through spring and summer, once a week in fall, and once a month in winter. You can water smaller plants in smaller containers somewhat more, but not much more. A good rule of thumb is: When you see plants in active growth, that is, fresh green shoots, give ample moisture. But when plants are resting do not try to force them into growth; it won't work, and you will lose the plant from overwatering. Always use tepid water because cold water shocks plants. And if possible, water in the morning so plants can dry out somewhat before evening. However, this is not dogma; I have a friend who waters his plants in the evening and they still grow. Also remember that clay pots dry out faster than plastic or glazed ones and that plants in dry sunny locations will need more water than those in only bright light. However, when in doubt, *do not water*. Keep jungle cacti such as *Epiphyllums, Rhipsalis*; Christmas and Easter cactus, moist all year.

In the author's living room, these cacti thrive. They receive good light and grow with minimum care, soil replenished every second year. Behind the sofa is *Cephalocereus*; at the fireplace, a *Cereus* cactus. (*Photo by Matthew Barr*)

FEEDING AND RESTING

Do not be brainwashed into thinking that all plants require feeding to make them grow. This will make the chemical manufacturers grow but not the plant, especially cacti. The only exception to this rule is specimen plants—those that have been in very large pots for years—because soil is spent of nutrients. Supplemental feeding is necessary with specimen plants for continued growth and vigor. Fertilize plants once a month during the growing season with a weak solution of a fertilizer such as 5-10-10.

Most cacti at one time of the year (usually winter) need a short rest to regain strength for another period of growth. This hiatus in activity is essential to their well-being and a natural part of their life cycle. In winter try to give plants somewhat cooler temperatures (about 55°F.), and water soil just enough so it does not become caked. Do not feed or try to force plants into growth; the result will be abnormal growth and a possible loss of flowers in summer. The rest period generally lasts for about a month to 6 weeks, and the plant itself will tell you when it is ready for more water and warmer temperatures: you will see fresh growth and the plant will, in general, assume a more perky look.

Exceptions to the need for a winter rest are the shade-loving jungle cacti such as *Epiphyllums*, Christmas and Easter cacti, and *Rhipsalis*. These plants need, as mentioned, regular watering throughout the year.

7. Cacti-like Plants

The following plants are succulents, not cacti. Many resemble cacti so closely (*Euphorbias*, for example) that I have included them. Also, some are just too good to miss and make fine indoor accents. For example, *Agaves* and *Aloes* are without equal and can add great beauty to a home; they are really overlooked plants that deserve more attention. Like cacti, they are invariably tough and grow with little attention.

EUPHORBIAS

These are discussed first because so many of them resemble cacti. *Euphorbias* are generally of the columnar or tree type and ideal for dramatic accent that will last for several years without special attention. The plants need a bright but not necessarily sunny place. Grow them in a well-drained soil kept moderately moist all year except in winter, when a dry rest for about 6 weeks is most beneficial. *Euphorbias* tolerate low humidity and a wide range of temperatures.

Here are some of the better *Euphorbias* for indoors:

Euphorbia grandicornis. An absolutely striking plant with whorling branches and ribbed stems. The ribs are wavy and decorated with spines.

E. horrida. This looks like a barrel-shaped cactus. Has ribs and toothed crests, is tough, and can take neglect if necessary.

Euphorbia lactea is the tall plant; it looks very much like a cactus and culture is the same. (*USDA photo*)

72

E. ingens. A beauty, with candelabra-type growth. Stems are dark green wavy ribs. Ideal for an accent against a white wall.

E. obovalifolia. A tall, branching plant with four-sided branches. Very different and interesting.

E. milii or *E. splendens.* This is the popular "crown of thorns." Mature specimens are stunning, with tiny, bright green leaves and vibrant red flowers. It makes an excellent house plant, but beware of the spines; they are sharp and lethal.

We can not leave this group of plants without mentioning *E. pulcherrima*, known as poinsettia, our Christmas favorite. This well-known plant needs rather meticulous care to survive throughout the year and is not really a good house plant, but for seasonal color it is well liked.

AGAVES

This fascinating group of plants, from the Amaryllis family, has incredible foliage color. Some are gray-green, others are dark green, and some are almost slate gray, which makes them desirable as unique color accents for interiors. The plants have a rosette growth, and most are armed with spines on leaf edges. *Agaves* require large containers to look their best and need a sandy soil. Give them bright light and they will decorate your home for years. This group includes my favorite, the century plant, which was with me for ten years until my cat surreptitiously discovered the milky juice within the leaves and in time he finally harmed the plant.

Agave americana (century plant). A 6-foot rosette packed with sword-shaped toothed leaves. Good grower.

A. attentuata. Big and bold, with soft gray-green leaves to 5 feet across. Handsome in low white tub.

A. filifera. Olive-green leaves with curly threads at the margin. A good bright accent for room corners and attractive in shallow and cylindrical terra cotta pots.

A. parryi huachucensis. A magnificent plant that looks like a piece of granite sculpture; has a rosette of tightly packed leaves with black spines at edges. Stunning.

Another cactus look-alike is *Euphorbia ingens*, a bizarre but beautiful plant heavily armed with spines; it makes a fine decorative accent in a room. Behind it on the table is the Golden Barrel cactus, *Echinocactus grusonii*. (*Photo by Matthew Barr*)

Aloes too look a great deal like cacti and make fine window plants. The rosette growth makes them especially attractive. (*Photo by author*)

A. victoriae-reginae. The ultimate in sculptural beauty, with wedge-shaped dark, dark green leaves delicately etched with white lines. A stunner in the right setting.

ALOES

These plants are often confused with *Agaves* because they look somewhat like them. Native to Africa and Madagascar and members of the lily family, *Aloes* have different flowers. Some (not all) make good decorative plants, specifically the rosette plants of uniform growth; others become too straggly for indoors. Give plants a rich soil (not so much sand) and somewhat more sun than *Agaves*. *Aloes* require plenty of water in summer to prosper.

Aloe aristata. A small plant, rosette, about 6 inches in diameter. Leaves have soft white spines. Makes a good table decoration.

A. ferox. Large dense rosette. Glaucous spiny leaves. Good plant for shallow tubs.

A. striata. White-striped and spineless gray-green leaves. Can grow large and makes a good pot plant.

A. variegata. (partridge-breasted *Aloe*). Dense rosette with 5-inch leaves.

YUCCAS

These leafy plants are appearing more and more as house plants. They do not resemble cacti as closely as the other plants mentioned here, but they do have dense rosettes of sword-shaped leaves and make excellent colorful house plants. *Yuccas* require a rich soil and a bright place to prosper. They are not temperamental about temperatures and grow almost untended. For best decoration use them in ornamental tapered pots.

Yucca aloifolia (Spanish bayonet). Branching, with dark green, stiff leaves. Plants may be single trunked or branched and can grow tall, to 6 feet.

Y. glauca. Leaves are margined with white on this nearly stemless plant.

Y. recurvifolia. Blue-grey-green foliage makes this Yucca desirable. Usually branchless, with offsets at base to form a clump.

This lovely *Agave* has beautiful symmetry and grows for years with little care. It is a splendid house plant and armed with spines at leaf edges resembles a cactus. (*Photo by Joyce R. Wilson*)

Haworthias make fine house plants; they can be used in dish gardens or as window plants for spot accents. (*Photo by Joyce R. Wilson*)

Y. whipplei. Stemless, with clusters of gray-green sharp-pointed leaves. Can grow big and makes good room accent.

HAWORTHIAS

Haworthias, very easy to grow, are usually small plants. Most are spiny and resemble cacti. They tolerate shade and make excellent plants for indoors. Leaves are usually in rosettes, but the stems sometimes become elongated. Haworthias like rather cool temperature (60°F.) and a sandy soil with scant waterings. Excellent for table and dish gardens.

Haworthia angustifolia. Light green rosettes of pointed leaves.
H. fasciata. Good small plant with zebra-striped leaves in rosette growth.
H. limifolia. Slow-growing species, with triangular, dark brownish-green leaves with lines.
H. tessellata. Checkered lines on glossy green, pointed leaves; rosette growth.

GASTERIAS

These generally small plants are related to the *Aloes* in the lily family, with leaves in a fan shape, although some grow in rosettes as they age. Usually leaves are dark green mottled with light green or white; flowers are bell shaped on slender stems. *Gasterias* are tenacious plants and can tolerate shade and neglect without harm. Plants come from South Africa and need somewhat (but not too much) more moisture than desert-type cacti.

Gasteria lilliputana. A lovely small plant, with dark green and pale green leaves; spiral growth.
G. maculata. Eight-inch mottled leaves with white spots or bands.
G. verrucosa. Tapered pink and purple leaves with white tubercles.

STAPELIAS

Inhabiting dry regions of Africa and the East Indies, these are bizarre but beautiful succulents. Plants are small and branched at the base. Flowers are incredible complexities of nature, large, and bloom indoors. Plants need warmth by day but some coolness at night; give them some shade in summer. Grow *Stapelias* in a rich soil.

Stapelia gigantea. Stems are 8 inches tall, with small spines on edges. Gigantic 12- to 14- inch bizarre flowers.

S. grandiflora. Angled stems, compressed, almost winglike, with soft hairs. Large flowers.

S. variegata. Gray-green stems, angled and armed with spines. Flowers are 2 to 5 inches across.

8. Starting New Plants and Protecting Those You Have

Once you have a few cacti at the windows or as indoor decoration you might want to multiply your favorite plants by *propagation*. The process is simple, although the word propagation makes it sound complex. Actually, many cacti have a branching habit, so you can merely take cuttings from your own plants and start them into growth. Dividing plants is another easy way to increase stock, as is using offsets (adventitious growth). Growing cacti from seed is still another way to get new plants—many of them—for little cost. This process is somewhat more exacting than taking a cutting and involves more time, but there is a certain satisfaction in growing your own plants from seed. Also, because some varieties are difficult to obtain, starting plants from seed is the only way to ensure getting the plant you want.

Protecting plants from insects and diseases is necessary but not difficult; all it takes is close observation to catch trouble before it starts. But even if you happen to be negligent (and who isn't at one time or another) and insects do attack plants, there are ways to get rid of them without much fuss.

CUTTINGS AND OFFSETS

These propagation processes are so simple that even a child can do them. Simply remove a joint of a branching cactus such as *Epiphyllum* or *Opuntia* and start it into growth in a propagating mix. Make a clean cut, and then let the surface form a callus (dry out). In a few days put the cutting (callus side down) in a sandy mix in a shallow container. Moisten the growing medium, and put a Baggie over the

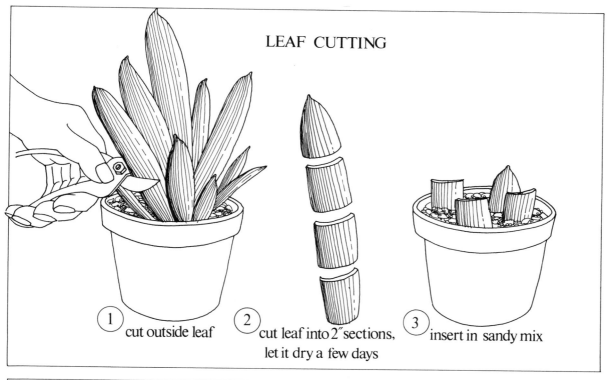

LEAF CUTTING

① cut outside leaf

② cut leaf into 2″ sections, let it dry a few days

③ insert in sandy mix

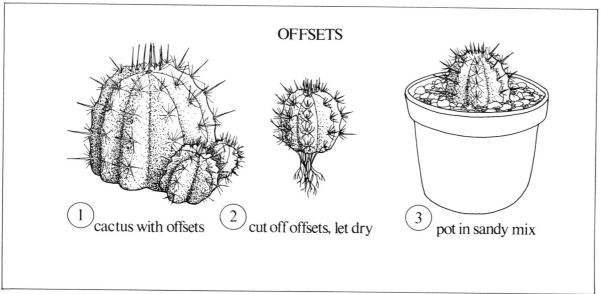

OFFSETS

① cactus with offsets

② cut off offsets, let dry

③ pot in sandy mix

Propagation

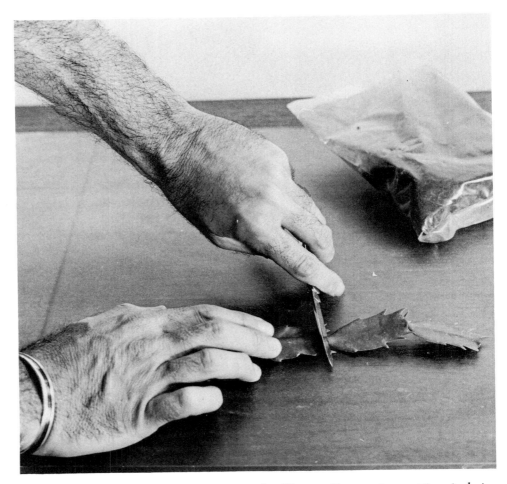

Taking a cutting from a cactus is simple. Here a *Zygocactus* cutting is being readied for planting. (*Photo by Matthew Barr*)

container to ensure good humidity. Keep temperatures somewhat warm (75°F.). When you notice signs of growth the cutting has taken root and can be potted separately in a soil mix. The best time to take cuttings is in May and June.

A great many cacti produce offsets at the base of the plant; offsets are miniature versions of the parent plants, sometimes with roots. *Echinopsis, Parodias, Lobivias* and *Mammillarias* frequently produce these baby plants. Remove the baby plant and pot it separately. With columnar cactus such as *Trichocereus* a slightly dif-

After cutting has dried for a day it is inserted in a mixture of soil and vermiculite. Plastic bag will be put over top to insure humidity. (*Photo by Matthew Barr*)

ferent method has to be used to get new plants. When the plant gets too tall, cut off the upper portion (about 4 inches) and set it into a sandy soil to start a new plant.

SEED
Packaged cactus seeds, available from suppliers, should be started in spring or at least early summer so they have a chance to grow before cold weather starts. For sowing seed use shallow containers

like azalea pots or, if necessary, glass baking dishes. A growing medium of 2 parts soil, 1 part leaf mold, and 2 parts clean sand is fine. You can also use vermiculite (sold in packages at nurseries) to start seed. Be sure the container has some drainage facilities so that excess water can escape. Pack the growing medium in the container. Do not pack it in tightly; just gently firm it in place. Allow room at the top of the container so there will be space to water.

To sow seed bury them twice their own diameter in the mix. Put the seed pans in a warm (78°F.) and bright place but without direct sun. Cover the containers with plastic or a Baggie, but if the plastic sweats too much, occasionally remove it so air can circulate in the container. Keep temperatures constant, and be sure the growing mix is always evenly moist. To water the seeds use a fine overhead mix or set the container in pans of water so soil can soak up moisture. The idea is not to disturb or wash away the seed. Too much moisture and darkness will bring on mildew, a bacterial rot, and with too little water the seeds simply will not germinate, so watering is of prime importance.

Some seeds will germinate quickly, but others might take months and, in a few cases, a year. Germination—the actual sprouting of the seed—depends on even temperature and moisture, season, and climate.

Once seeds have sprouted new leaves, give them somewhat more light, and remove the plastic covering. A good circulation of air and light are important now to get seedlings into growth. Keep soil evenly moist, and observe young plants frequently to see they are getting on all right. It takes about 6 months to a year before plants will be ready for new containers.

Plant Problems
Your cacti will rarely be invaded by insects or disease because they are tough plants and if well grown remarkably resistant to ills. If a plant is not doing well, do not immediately think insects are the cause. Many times culture is the culprit. Yellowing of the foliage or green stems that turn brown are cultural problems, not insects or disease. Study the following chart before you run out and buy insecticides.

Dividing a plant takes a few minutes. Here the section of plant is being separated from the parent plant. Pot it up in a sandy soil and give it adequate light and humidity. Presto! . . . two plants from one. (*Photo by Matthew Barr*)

COMMON AILMENTS AND HOW TO COPE WITH THEM

Symptom	Probable Cause	Remedy
Failure to make new growth	Too much water or soil is compacted; roots may be decayed	Repot in fresh soil mixture; adjust watering practices
Stems or leaves are yellow	Plant is too dry and receives too much heat	Provide better ventilation and more moisture in the air
Stems or leaves *turn* yellow	Possible iron deficiency from soil being too alkaline	Test pH of soil; add iron chelates if reaction is neutral to alkaline
Pale color on new growth	Root injury	Trim away dead or damaged roots; repot plant
Elongated growth	Not enough light	Move plant to location with more light
Failure to bloom or very few flowers produced	Plant has received too much nitrogen, or winter rest period has not been given, or both	Use fertilizer low in nitrogen, higher in phosphorus; give plants winter rest
Flower buds drop	Temperature is too low or fluctuates too much; plant is in draft	Move plant to warmer, draft-free location

Offsets from plants can be severed with a sharp knife, dried for a day in the air and then potted up as individual plants. Dust the wound on the parent plant with charcoal. (*Photo by Matthew Barr*)

COMMON AILMENTS AND HOW TO COPE WITH THEM

Symptom	Probable Cause	Remedy
Soft or mushy growth	Too much moisture, temperature too low	Reduce moisture, cut away soft parts, and dust cuts with Captan
Corky skin on stems	A natural development on some cacti as they age	
Plant has glassy, translucent look beginning in fall or winter	Frost damage	No cure for damage done. Keep plant dry; be sure it is not subjected to such low temperatures again

As mentioned, it will be rare for plants to be attacked by insects, but if care is not the best, weak plants will be invaded by pests. The trick now is to identify the insect before you do anything. Generally, most insects are small and hard to see and they hide. You are most apt to find them clustered around the spines or needles, or even in the soil. You may not be able to see the insects at first glance, but you will know if they have appeared: plants may have discolored leaves and/or deformed growth of new shoots.

Here are the common insects you should know:

Aphids: Probably the most common pest you will find, these small green-to-black, soft-bodied creatures dine on tender growing shoots and flower parts, distorting the young growth. *Control*: nicotine sulfate or Malathion. Be sure plants are watered the day before applying the preparation, and keep plants shaded for a few hours after you spray.

Scale has attacked this cactus but has not done damage yet. Scale can be removed by picking off with a toothpick or by brushing off with a laundry soap solution. (*Photo by Matthew Barr*)

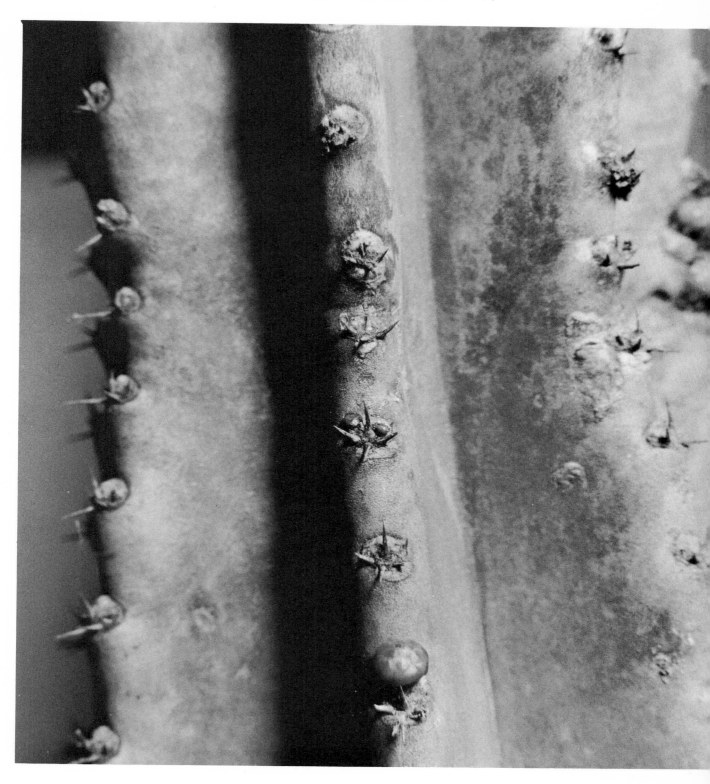

Mealybugs are a nemesis of cactus and have invaded the spines areas. Get rid of them quickly with alcohol on a cotton swab or use a house plant aerosal. (*Photo by Matthew Barr*)

Snails find cactus good fare. Inspect plants frequently to eliminate them. (*Photo by Matthew Barr*)

Mealybugs: These insects cause extensive plant damage unless found early. Fuzzy white or gray and cottony, these insects are found on the spines, stems, and roots of plants. *Control*: Spray with a weak solution of nicotine sulfate (Black Leaf 40) or with Diazinon.

Scale: This is a stubborn pest to eradicate; the insects look like brown spots about the size of a pinhead with a hard-shell covering. *Control*: If the infestation is mild, pick off scale with a toothpick. For heavy attacks you will have to resort to Malathion. Use with care exactly as prescribed in package.

Thrips and red spider: Clues to the presence of these insects are small yellow or white spots on leaves or stems. *Control*: Spray with nicotine sulphate (Black Leaf 40) or use solution of laundry soap and water applied frequently.

Snails and slugs: The work of these chewers is easily evidenced by holes and torn growth. Unfortunately, snails and slugs adore cacti but because they are readily visible, eliminating the pests is not difficult. *Control*: Use Cory's Slug and Snail Bait (at nurseries); scatter it over the soil and then water lightly.

DISEASE IN PLANTS

Disease in plants usually results from poor conditions and plain carelessness. Overwatering and improperly healed cuts are a few ways decay can start. Soft decayed areas and rot can also develop at the base of the plant if it is planted too deeply. Cut away the fungus-infected areas, then dust wounds with sulfur or a specific fungicide such as Captan.

Prevention is half the battle with plant diseases and this includes keeping the growing area clean at all times and keeping plants well groomed. Remove any dead leaves or flowers immediately and keep soil surface clean of debris.

9. *Some Popular Cacti*

In every plant family—African violets to philodendrons—some plants become more popular than others because of availability or because of their lovely flowers. In the cactus group, *Epiphyllums* and night-blooming *Cereus* species are well known for their dramatic flowers. Gift plants too, such as Easter cactus, Christmas cactus and Poinsettias, are long time favorites with their bowers of bloom.

There are also what are known as collectors' plants, that is, rare species that capture the fancy of plant enthusiasts, for example: flowering stones, *Mammillarias*, and *Gymnocalcyiums*.

THE BLOOMING BEAUTIES

Epiphyllums produce large saucerlike flowers in many colors and in July and August these are breath-taking plants. With flattened stems, spineless, there are more than 3,000 named varieties in stunning colors. As decorative accents for patio or garden room, *Epiphyllums* are tough to beat. The plants are also easy to grow and need very little care; furthermore, they will bear flowers even in filtered light. Grow them in a porous, well drained sandy soil and be sure that they have cool nights to encourage bloom (55°F.). In winter keep soil barely moist, and place them in an unheated but not freezing place (a garage or porch).

Pot *Epiphyllums* in small containers because they do best when roots are crowded. Let them dry out thoroughly between waterings. Repot only when absolutely necessary.

Some good hybrids include:

White, Cream, Yellow—Baby Doll; Polar Bear
Pink—Carnation; Flower Song; Princess Betty
Orange—Cherokee Chief; Keepsake; Sunland
Red—Bacchus; Cardinal; Fireside
Purple—Ceylon; Gertrude W. Beahm; Harmony

Other beautiful flowering cacti are the legendary night-blooming *Hylocereus* and *Selenicereus* plants. These are huge and can grow to 15 feet with flattened leaves, segmented, dark almost gray-green. They resemble overgrown *Epiphyllums*, in bloom they are stunning although flowers last but a scant 24 to 36 hours. Because they require so little care they are worth their keep (if you have space) the rest of the year.

Hylocereus undatus is most commonly seen. This beauty has deep green triangular leaves and immense scented flowers. *H. triangularis* and *H. polyrhizus* are similar and also desirable.

Selenicereus macdonaldiae is sometimes called "Queen of the Night" and has long, trailing stems. The incredible white flowers are often more than 12 inches across. *S. grandiflorus* is similar and equally beautiful in bloom.

Harrisia, sometimes called *Eriocereus*, are other fine flowering cacti. Plants in this group grow more upward then pendent and thus can be more easily accommodated in limited space. Generally, these plants have nocturnal flowers.

GIFT PLANTS

You are probably familiar with the Christmas and Easter cactus. Years ago, it seemed as if everyone had one at the window sill. *Schlumbergera gaertneri*, formerly called Easter cactus, is lovely with pink or red flowers, hundreds on a well-grown plant. If you receive one of these plants try to keep it growing all year for in time it becomes stunning. The Christmas cactus, *Zygocactus truncatus* is equally handsome and many new hybrids have been developed that bloom abundantly in the season.

Orchid cactus known as *Epiphyllums* are popular plants because they have lovely, large flowers. (*Photo by author*)

To keep these gift plants in the home put them in a cool but bright place after you get them. Keep soil evenly moist. In summer, try them outdoors where they will benefit from refreshing rains and good air circulation. After Labor Day, return them to their window place and continue to grow them in good light. In the evening find a cool spot for them. To get the plants to bud, starting in October give them 12 to 14 hours of total darkness for about 45 days. (Even a street lamp near a window will prevent bud formation.) In the middle of December or sooner return them to a bright warm place where you can appreciate the flowers.

The Christmas poinsettia, *Euphorbia pulcherrima*, is a succulent (not a cactus), and this is a favorite gift plant. Unfortunately, it is difficult to keep through the years indoors. It resents hot, dry atmosphere and likes coolness at night (55°F.). It also needs a summer outdoors to really prosper and then repotting in early fall for the new season.

In recent years new hybrids of the poinsettia have been developed that are better suited to home conditions and that hold their flowers over a long period. These are the Mikkelson hybrids. If your local nursery does not have them, they are worth the search because they do provide abundant bloom in winter when most plants are without flowers.

COLLECTOR'S PLANTS

GYMNOCALYCIUM. This genus is included because recently plants have appeared in many flower shops and at Woolworths, sometimes masquerading under the erroneous name "moon plants." Either way, these are amenable plants, mostly globular with few ribs. Some have short spines, others long spines. Even out of flower the spine formation is attractive. Because plants flower even when young they make excellent decorative indoor subjects. Further, all these beauties need is a well-drained, rich soil. They will even fare well in bright light rather than the sunniest place.

G. baldianum. This one grows to about 3 inches in diameter with

Night-blooming *Cereus* are old time favorites. This is one of author's plants, many years old. (*Photo by author*)

short, spreading, radial spines. The flowers are usually dark red or sometimes pink.

G. mihanovichii. This is a variable species but generally it has defined ribs and is grayish-green with radial spines long and curved. The plant is small, about 2 inches, and fine for dish gardens. The flowers are usually greenish-yellow. Cultivars of this plant called *G. mihanovichii var. friedrichii* ''Ruby Ball' have appeared everywhere for sale.

G. multiflorum. While not as floriferous as most *Gymnocalyciums*, this species is robust and grows with almost no care.

G. shickendantzii. A pretty plant with spiral ribs covered with stout spines. The flowers are greenish and attractive. Easy to grow.

MAMMILLARIA. *Mammillarias* have long been favorites of cacti enthusiasts and they are included here because some of them make excellent house plants. There is a great variety in habit of growth; some are cluster plants, large, while others never exceed 3 or 4 inches. Also, to add to their desirability, a great many are fast growing compared to most cacti, which may take 5 or 10 years to mature.

Most *Mammillarias* are low growing and without ribs. Spines may be short and stiff or hairy and featherlike. The small flowers appear at the crown of the plant in circlets and are formed on previous years' growth; colors are cream or yellow, sometimes red. No matter which plant you choose (and there are some 300 different kinds) you are bound to have an attractive addition to the window or table garden.

The following species are some of the easier fast-growing types:

M. bocasana. This is one of the most popular which rapidly clusters to form cushions. They are bluish-green and covered with silky white spines. In late spring yellow flowers are borne in abundance. An excellent window plant that will need good moisture in summer and even in winter some water so soil doesn't become caked.

M. candida. This is included because it is so beautiful if not so easily cultivated. Its problem is that it is intolerant of water at the base so take precautionary measures. The plant is spherical and densely clothed in white silky spines. Flowers appear in early summer; they are white and numerous. Keep somewhat dry most of the time.

Epiphyllum flowers are big and colorful, at peak bloom in August. (*Photo by author*)

A hybrid Easter cactus resplendent with pink flowers. (*Photo by author*)

M. elongata. Perhaps this is not the prettiest *Mammillaria* but it grows quickly and with little care. The plant has finger-shaped clusters and creamy flowers appear in early spring if the plant is placed on a windowsill.

M. hahniana. This s a variable species but generally it is grayish-green with long hairs. Its chief attraction for me are the reddish-purple flowers that do bloom indoors in summer.

M. rhodantha. A very popular plant because it is so easy to grow. Varying from rich red to varying shades of brown and yellow, the spines are the attraction. The flowers are magenta red in summer.

M. Schiedeana. A very pretty *Mammillaria* and now being seen more often. This is a clustering plant, dark green and covered with

Mammillarias are favorite collector's plants; this one is at peak bloom. (*Photo courtesy Johnson Cactus Gardens*)

golden spines. It never grows too large and if you keep it on the dry side will be an asset at any place in a room.

FLOWERING STONES. These incredible plants are the favorites of many collectors. They are amazing replicas of tiny pebbles and stones and grow in the dry areas of South Africa. They have two pairs of fleshy leaves that act as water reservoirs and grow low on the ground. Because they have no spines or thorns their camouflage is their only defense against being eaten by animals. Only when flowering stones are in bloom are they easily distinguishable.

Almost 20 genera have flowering stone plants; perhaps the most popular genus is *Pleiospilos*. Plants are small and grow in clusters. *P. bolusii* and *P. nelii* are perhaps most popular. *Lithops*, another genus, have flat-topped leaves separated by a cleft. *L. hallii* and *L. karasmontana* are sometimes seen. *Conophytums* and *Fenestraria* are also in this group.

For indoor culture, flowering stones grow best in a very fine soil mixture of equal parts sand and soil. Be sure containers have ample drainage facilities because standing water quickly deteriorates plants. The plants need warmth and bright light but must never be over-watered; even once could mean disaster. A group of flowering stones in a decorative container is always a conversation piece in the home. Plants must be ordered from mail-order specialists.

10. A Yearly Guide to Cacti Care

The part of the country you live in will greatly affect your plants, but generally there are certain cultural practices that apply anywhere, which is what this chapter is all about.

JANUARY

This is usually a resting time for most cacti but not for the epiphytic types like *Zygocactus*, *Schlumbergera*, and *Rhipsalis*. These plants will be in bloom now and will thus require watering at least once a week, perhaps more.

Try to maintain moderate temperatures for plants, 60°F. minimum at night. Remember these rules are only for the cacti just mentioned; other species will enjoy lower temperatures (50°F.) and very little moisture, just enough to prevent soil from caking. Be sure there is adequate ventilation for plants, and on sunny mornings mist plants but very lightly; by night all moisture should be gone or plants will be apt to rot.

Sow some seed now. Select your favorite species, and start them under artificial light or in warm, protected, bright locations.

FEBRUARY

February is an erratic month weatherwise, but plants will be getting more sun as the days lengthen. Species from the genera *Rebutia* and *Lobivia* may be starting to show flower buds. Start watering moderately so plants can begin growing again after their winter hiatus.

Repot plants that need it; overgrown plants in small pots are rarely attractive, and plants need more room to grow and fresh nutrients from new soil to thrive.

Be sure potting soils are mixed and ready to use and that containers are sterilized. Scrub containers with scalding water and Brillo pads and then rinse them in clear water. Check plant labels and names: Study cacti catalogs so you can start ordering those species you especially want.

With a small fork aerate dry, caked soil; simply dig the top inch or so. At the end of the month start to increase moisture for plants.

March

You may not be able to see spring in any visible content outdoors, but if you are observant indoors you will notice the first signs of spring in your cacti. Many will be starting into growth, which is your sign to start watering more frequently and to increase temperatures to 78°F. during the day. Normally, this temperature will occur in most average home conditions.

Repot any plant that needs it. Use the next-sized container (standard pots are sold in 2-inch increments). Never use an overly large pot for cacti because soil can turn sour and harm plants.

Globular cacti should be coming into bloom with little buds showing, and generally most plants will be perking up in the additional spring warmth and sunshine. Water plants about once a week, but do not drench plants or get water on them. An exception is on sunny days, when you can provide a light mist as long as plants dry by evening.

April

Continue to repot plants that need it; warm weather will encourage new growth. All cacti except *Conophytums* and *Lithops* can receive regular watering now. Be sure to provide more humidity (put plants on gravel trays or mist area lightly). The atmosphere for plants should be buoyant, so be sure there is air circulation in the growing area. Spring-flowering species will start to show buds.

Because the sun is stronger now watch plants closely to see whether they are being scorched. Dark brown or black areas indicate the plant is being burned by the sun. Apply necessary shading; sometimes all that is needed is a light curtain at the window.

With warmer weather there are apt to be more insects around. Inspect plants, especially for mealy bug. Eliminate any you find by dabbing them with cotton swabs dipped in alcohol.

MAY

May will show an increase in growth of all plants. Because of higher temperatures, more water will be necessary. Keep soil evenly moist, and give your plants as much light as possible.

Many varieties will be coming into flower, so apply water once a week, more often if the weather is really warm. Fresh air is still a necessary requirement for good health; open windows near plants, but protect them from drafts. Keep on the lookout for insects; catching trouble before it starts is half the battle in the war against plant pests.

This is a good time to start cuttings from old plants that may be in bad shape.

JUNE

The routine is much the same as for May: Give moderate but thorough watering and provide good ventilation. Do not get water on flower buds or they may rot. Increase humidity as mentioned. Plants need good humidity, at least 30 to 50 percent.

Some cacti can be put in the garden now to enjoy the refreshing June rains and good sunlight. Move pot and all and put it in a sunny location. However, be sure that plants like *Epiphyllums*, *Haworthias*, *Gasterias*, and *Rhipsalis* have some protection from direct sun; they do best in bright light.

Remove any plants that are not growing. If they are not bothered by insects, move the plant to a different place. Sometimes an inch or so one way or the other will put the plant in the right place where it will grow.

JULY

During this very hot month your plants will need good watering and a buoyant atmosphere. Be sure the air is not stagnant or red spider may develop and ruin a plant. If this pest does strike, use a laundry soap–and–water solution several times a week to get rid of them.

Again, watch plants for leaf scorch; July sun can be blazing even indoors. The plants you repotted in early spring should be showing good growth by now. Be sure they have plenty of humidity and even moisture for the soil.

AUGUST

Routine is very much the same as for July, but some plants— *Epiphyllums* especially—should be starting their rest time. For these plants, just keep soil barely moist.

If you missed repotting plants in spring, August is another good time to do it. Plants will have an excellent chance to start growth before cool weather starts. If you have previously shaded plants from direct summer sun, you can remove shading now.

SEPTEMBER

In areas with severe winters, September is the time to start tapering off water. If the weather is dull and cool, water plants once every 10 days. If it is unseasonably hot, water more often.

Remove plants that have not responded during the year, and discard them if you can bear it. Shop for new plants because there is still time for them to get accustomed to new conditions before real winter weather starts.

At the end of the month, sometimes sooner, depending upon where you live, return any plants from outdoors and move them to their display places in the house. Be sure they are free of garden insects; inspect pots thoroughly. Reduce temperatures somewhat because many species will soon be starting their resting times.

OCTOBER

Stop watering routinely most globular cacti, but continue light waterings for others. Remove any shading because now plants can take full light. Remove dead leaves so mildew does not have a chance to start. To get your Christmas cacti varieties in bud, set them in a dark place (absolutely no light), and keep them just barely moist. These plants need a 7- to 8-week dark period, that is, 14 hours of darkness per day to initiate flower buds.

Be alert for sudden frosts, and protect your favorite plants by moving them away from windows.

November

Most cacti (other than epiphytic ones) will now be starting their rest period. This does not mean complete abandonment on your part; just keep soil barely damp to the touch. Give plants lower light levels as they go through their dormancy—naturally, light will be diminished with winter weather, as will temperature, which is just fine. Most cacti will do well at, say, 50°F. during the winter rest.

Clean up the growing area or groom display plants meticulously because the Christmas season, with guests coming into the home, is on the way. Look over books about your favorite plant; the more you learn about them the more you will appreciate their beauty.

December

Return Christmas cacti to a bright place, and start watering them to encourage good bud formation. Do not turn plants because buds are sensitive to light and will fall off.

Other cacti are resting so there is little work for you to do. But since now is the holiday season, sit back and relax and enjoy your cacti.

Where to Buy Plants

Cacti are available at nurseries and patio shops as well as Woolworth-type stores as described in chapters 5 and 9. The following is a list of mail order suppliers. It is not meant to be a complete list but rather those companies I have dealt with or known about through the years.

Abbey Gardens
P.O. Box 167
Reseda, CA 91335

Wide selection of cacti and succulents.

Beahm Gardens
2686 Paloma
Pasadena, CA 91107

Epiphyllums and related plants.

Cactus Gem Nursery
P.O. Box 327
Aromas, CA 95004

Good selection of cacti and succulents.

Cactus by Mueller
10411 Rosedale Hwy.
Bakersfield, CA 93308

Good selection.

Grigsby Cactus Gardens
2354 Bella Vista Dr.
Vista, CA 92083

50 cents for catalog.

Henrietta's Nursery
1345 N. Brawley
Fresno, CA 93705

Very extensive selection
of all kinds of cacti.
20 cents for catalog.

Merry Gardens
Camden, MN 04843

Small but good selection
of cacti.

Books to Read

This is a short reading list on cacti; there are dozens of books on the subject. These books have been chosen because they are the ones I am most familiar with.

Edgar and Brian Lamb, *Cacti and Other Succulents*, 4 volumes. London: Blandford Press, Ltd., 1968.

Walter Haage, *Cacti and Succulents*. London: Studio Vista Books, 1965.

Margaret J. Martin, P.R. Chapman, and H.A. Auger, *Cacti and Their Cultivation*. London: Faber & Faber, 1972. First American edition, Winchester Press, 1972.

Vera Higgins, *Cacti for Decoration*. London: Blandford Press Ltd., 1956.

Martha Van Ness, *Cacti and Succulents, Indoors and Out*. Van Nostrand Reinhold, Inc., 1971.

Claude Chismian, *The Book of Cacti and other Succulents*. New York: Doubleday & Co., 1958.

S.H. Scott, *The Observer's Book of Cacti and Other Succulents*. London and New York: Frederick Warne & Co., Ltd., 1958.